IT IS YOUR TIME TO SHINE

A Personal Branding Formula to Build Your Influence

SAMAR M. BAQER

ISBN: 978-1-948777-30-8

Acknowledgment

I would like to express my gratitude and appreciation to every person in my life who supported my journey and encouraged me to stay strong and hopeful. Special thanks to my husband who did all he can for this book to see the light. Thank you, my love, for putting up with me and for always believing in my success. This book is dedicated to those who want to be change agents in the world. The ones who do not complain about problems, but rather create solutions. The ones who should show up and shine.

Contents

Introduction

When I decided to write a book, I wanted it to be inspirational and impactful to all kinds of people. In my country, I am known as a marketing professor and an expert in my field. While all of my friends and colleagues thought that I would write a marketing textbook to be used for teaching purposes, I knew that this kind of project would not satisfy my hunger for serving others, especially the younger generations of today. Something inside of me wanted to reach a different target, a target beyond the walls of the classroom. I wanted to help others while also feeding my own soul with what I love doing most; public speaking, educating, and training.

I come from Kuwait, a small but beautiful country in the Middle East. Known for its strong support of different countries and entities across the world, giving and serving others are amongst the deepest values that I was raised upon. Having all of my traditions and cultural values in mind, I built my career and image through hard work and persistence, which I am very proud of. Coming up on my 15th year of academic work at my university, I have dedicated my energy to both teaching and inspiring my students, consistently bringing that same sense of enthusiasm to the multiple trainings and speaking engagements I've participated in throughout my working years.

As a personal branding trainer, clients usually approach me with feelings of confusion regarding their brand. The biggest question I get has to do with process; clients are usually unsure if they should start their business before marketing it as an entity, or if they should begin by marketing themselves as brands prior to marketing their business. Most of the time, they are service providers such as doctors and lawyers. My first question to them is always, "Are you sure you can handle being famous?" In general, most clients respond by providing every single reason that fame scares them; they like the glamour aspect, but they are not sure they're prepared for it.

With the exponential growth of social media platforms, there are many unqualified individuals who have become famous and started to guide the young generations. It breaks my heart to see how many of these influencers have led today's youth in the wrong directions. When I was growing up, I had many local and international role models that I used to—and still do—look up to. From Zuhoor, my first grade Physical Education teacher who was always happy and full of energy, to Christine Lagarde, the current president of the European Central Bank and an indomitable lawyer and business figure, I have had no shortage of mentors to admire and follow. Despite my conservative origins, there was always a big dream guiding me to my future as I developed into a strong and independent woman and leader.

Thanks to the media, today's concept of a role model has changed. Younger generations are looking at individuals who have achieved easy and fast wealth, which doesn't make much logical sense. Many teenagers are losing their self-confidence because they feel that they are not good enough, smart enough, or even pretty enough to have a hope for the future. They are Surrounded by false, unrealistic idols, many teenagers today are left with beaten-down self-confidence, feeling that they are not as good, smart, or even pretty as they should be.

If you are a parent or a parental figure to a teenager, have you ever complained because your child follows social influencers 24 hours a day? Have you ever felt worried that they are changing their behavior to mirror those influencers? Have you seen young girls looking for plastic surgeons to alter their looks to mirror their favorite celebrities?

Don't get me wrong, I am not against social media, nor influencers; there are lessons we can learn about how this unique social landscape is facilitating the marketing process in a wonderful way. I am worried, however, that these social media influencers—and, to many, role models—are planting materialism in the brains of today's youth.

I believe that we should not blame teenagers for having this ultimate dream to become an influencer. We can only blame ourselves. When I say "we," I mean us, professionals, the ones who have worked hard and smart to reach our goals with booming success stories. The ones who *made it*, despite life's obstacles and hardships. Some grew up suffering from domestic abuse, discrimination, chronic illness, trauma, or a tragic accident, but we made it in our own way, some of us acquiring both fame and wealth in the process. However, we failed to mentor and guide those more junior than us. We were busy, distracted and maybe too proud to be in media all the time. We were not quick enough to utilize the new technology that currently serves younger generations. With that being said, I wholeheartedly believe that it is our responsibility to take them back to their roots, and to provide a picture of "good famous." We must stress the relevance of figures like Tony Robbins, Oprah Winfrey, Brendon Burchard, and Lisa Nichols; individuals who share stories of perseverance, hope, and gratitude to connect with those who can benefit from their experience and wisdom.

Younger generations are hungry for inspiration, especially on a global scale. A young girl in Africa, Latin America, or the Middle East needs to see someone from her own culture, exemplifying success and development. She can easily find someone to teach her how to apply makeup or fix her hair, but she must consistently search for someone to show her how to build a career with dignity and passion. You get my point, right?

Imagine that successful entrepreneurs, doctors, and other inspiring individuals are motivating your kids, or even you, to build more skills that will carry them forward. Imagine that you are that person who is brimming with motivation every single day to lead future generations. Wouldn't that be amazing?

That's the exact thing that motivated me to write this book. I want to offer you a strategy that will encourage you to create a personal brand and prepare you for what you might face in the process.

Similar books in today's current landscape talk about the best marketing techniques and branding strategies to attract your target market and collect a million followers on Instagram. However, that is not the main objective of this book. In laying the foundation of your brand, you deserve *real* preparation to support your budding foundation, honest guidance that will help you on your journey to success, and thorough coaching to build your position as an influencer and a "good famous" public figure.

I decided to write this book not just to guide you in marketing yourself, but also to humbly participate in encouraging people everywhere to spread their light in our societies and provide amazing role models to the young generation of today.

This book will show you how to dig deeper in your life and find the real anchor for your brand. It will discuss all obstacles that are stopping you from showing up and help you to overcome them. You will learn about the formula that will prepare you for standing out in your field. I personally went through each element of this formula. It's simple and obvious, but as Brendon Burchard says, "Common sense is not always common practice." We just need someone to direct our attention to the obvious and make it our practice.

Once you apply the formula, you will start to have a clear idea about your own personal brand. It is the first and most important step that will lead you to the success you deserve. Whether you want to teach people how to properly practice yoga, or you want to inspire them to survive cancer, this book will prepare you for that moment when you write the first blog post, the first Instagram post, or shoot the first video.

There is nothing better than serving the universe with your gift and your talents. Every person you inspire, every teenager you motivate, and every lost soul you empower, will bring you feelings of peace and satisfaction beyond words.

ONE

Stand on Your Story

"You are the designer of your destiny; you are the author of your story."

Lisa Nichols

Your Story Makes You Unique

No matter how young or old we are, how poor or how rich, or even how successful we are, we all have special experiences that shape our personalities. Some of us have interesting and unique stories, while others may have life tales full of joy or riddled with sadness, but all narratives are full of wisdom and priceless lessons. We go through life meeting people on a daily basis, some of whom add hope to our lives, while others cause us pain, but with each passing day, we learn from these individuals and we build on what we have learned to create our unique realities. Our experiences and emotions are extremely powerful, crafting strong building blocks for our life narratives. In many cases, the power of our stories can impact our circle of friends, family, or even those that we have never met.

There is not a single successful businessperson that has not experienced hardships and struggles. For example, an active humanitarian who visits the poorest countries to help those in need is filled with memories and messages that awaken the materialistic world. A cardiologist has dealt with many impactful moments while performing operations, either curing their patients, or losing them. An immigrant has seen the face of death, facing poverty and hunger before reaching the borders of a hosting country, only to become a successful entrepreneur.

Special Success Stories Are Not Only Related to Business

Some of you might think "Well, I am not a doctor or a professional, so why I do need a personal brand?" A personal brand is not intended exclusively for entrepreneurs and other professionals. Even a mother who is struggling to raise her kids can have the best personal brand to help other mothers just like her around the world.

Upon reading this book, you will discover that while some stories that may look simple and ineffective, it's important to remember that each and every life experience can change your destiny, guide you to your life's purpose and help you succeed in defining your own personal brand.

Identifying The Story

Some of my clients used to say, " Samar, I have so many stories and I don't know which one to use." If you are lucky and have a life full of adventures and experiences, then the answer is easy!

To start, you need to think deeply about your purpose and the value you offer. What is the message that you are uniquely qualified to deliver to the universe? The story you will pick should be a direct representation of your purpose. Secondly, you should identify the relevance to your audience. How will hearing your story benefit others in their own situations? Finally, you should pick the story that you feel comfortable sharing with your audience with complete and utter honesty and pride. This is where being vulnerable comes into play;

remember that while sharing your story with an audience, you will be representing their fears, dreams, hopes, and more.

Step 1 | Discovering Your Purpose

Believe it or not, this is the most critical step to figuring out your story. Have you ever felt that you're just going through life without really knowing the mission you were meant for? Some are lucky to know their purpose from their childhood. When I watch an interview with one of these kinds of people, and they say things like, "I always knew that I would help by saving lives," or "I was born to own and run multiple businesses," I'm always completely fascinated, as you may be as well. You may think, *God! They are really lucky. I wonder if they'll ever question their purpose at later stages in their lives.*

I went through my questioning phase when I turned 40 years old. I had this haunting fear that I might die without knowing my true purpose and mission. Something was calling for me to search for my purpose, telling me that this was the right time. If anyone looked at my life at that time, they would think that I already had the perfect scenario; a well-known and respected professor who owns many beautiful and luxurious items and was building her dream house with her wonderful husband. Yet, there was a void within my soul, one that I could not quite identify. I realized that each and every day, I was simply doing my job and keeping my obligations at home and at work; there was no passion or challenge in my daily routine. I was missing my purpose. Many years ago, I thought that my purpose was to receive a PhD degree and return to my country to educate others and work on academic research. I didn't know that what I was calling my "purpose" was just a major step in my journey of living the bigger purpose. That is the moment when I started to hunt for my "true" purpose.

Of course, as you embark on your journey, you are bound to run into some discouraging friends and family members. They see your perfect picture scenario from the outside, but they do not understand your inner struggles or hardships. In terms of my own path, I knew that my family and friends cared about me and did not want to see me sad and confused, but I knew I could not listen to them. They saw me as a strange and ungrateful soul who felt depressed and could not enjoy what she already has. I stopped listening to them; deep down, I was certain of my gratitude for everything that God has given me, and I just wanted to serve more. I was simply looking to do my original job as part of this beautifully created universe.

To help me in my journey, I searched YouTube and various web pages for videos and articles that could help provide me with some direction. While doing so, I started to see patterns in my life; what I do very well and what I do consistently.

As part of my search, I found a Ted Talk by Pastor Rick Warren about his book *The Purpose Driven Life*. At first, I thought it was another religious lecture that would not interest me, especially since the subject manner was about a religion that I do not follow. But for some reason, I kept watching, as Pastor Warren began to talk about the story of Moses. The Quran contains the same story—one I have read many times—but this was the first time that I looked at it from an amazing new perspective. When God asked Moses about his staff, he wanted him to pay attention to the blessing that had already been given to him. Pastor Warren explained that the staff represented Moses's identity as a shepherd, his source of income, and his influence.

This was mind-blowing for me; a comparison that was so easy and obvious, but one that I had never identified. The staff was always there for him; it was his tool that helped him do his job and it was his miracle that aided him in manifesting his prophecy.

It taught me that our purpose is something that we are already doing. It is in our hands. We have a tendency to make things more complicated and to look elsewhere for answers, even if the solution is right in front of us. Some of us take a long time to discover our purpose, while others realize it from childhood, but our purpose is a built-in gift granted to us by God.

After watching this video, I started to look for my own staff. Was it teaching? Was it training? Was it being in academia? I asked my family, friends, and work colleagues to describe me in three words, specifically from a professional perspective. I didn't care if they told me that I have OCD or that I am stubborn or sweet; I wanted them to describe the professional woman that they see and know. Upon receiving their answers, I was surprised to learn that many of my colleagues mentioned that I am a great speaker; when I speak or get into a conversation, they like to listen to me. They also responded by telling me that I am a logical person who uses analytical thinking. *Bingo*. Message received, loud and clear.

Back then, in addition to my job, I was leading a lot of trainings, including consultations and various coaching services. Thanks to the feedback from my peers, I finally identified my purpose; to educate and inspire others. My place was—and still is—on the speaking stage to teach and motivate people. I had never truly paid attention to the level of happiness that I get from speaking on a stage; of course I get nervous, but my energy escalates and I keep going, staying confident in the message I am conveying.

I was happy to discover the obvious as it took me awhile to appreciate my talents and calling in life. I am a born educator and trainer, even teaching and educating my fellow primary school classmates when I was young. I was always the person my family would go to for advice, feeling assured that I would keep their secrets safe. And when it comes to standing on a stage and facing an audience, I am fearless, no matter the size of my audience.

This is my story. I have many others, but this is the one that I will always use to help people find their purpose. As I mentioned earlier, this is the most critical step. Even if you're a skillful lawyer or interior designer, you need to identify your story, the one that's attached to your purpose in some way. Your story is the connector and channel that will facilitate the practice of your purpose and mission. Find the story that's linked to your purpose so that you can create the personal brand that will bring your light and allow you to show up.

Step 2 | *Identify Your Audience: You Are a Solution To a Problem*

After knowing your purpose, you should start to identify your audience, whether that be patients, clients, cancer survivors, mothers or another specific group of individuals. We will discuss ways to identify your audience in further detail in chapters to come, but most importantly, you need to understand the problems or the needs that they have. There has to be a connection between your purpose and your story, and the emotional and physical needs of your clients.

Let's say that you are a physical therapist. You've struggled with an injury that you have had since childhood, but you managed to overcome its effect with your hard work and persistence. For years, you fought the pain while helping others with similar struggles. Your story of overcoming your hardship helped you identify your purpose in life; freeing others from pain caused by sudden injuries. Your patients will always relate to your story because while telling them about your story, you are explaining the same situation that they are facing or have faced. They will listen to you, they will trust you, and they will see the solution and the end of their pain.

Step 3 | Be Honest, Vulnerable, and Authentic

If you are a successful entrepreneur, you most likely have a strong sense of pride in your accomplishments, resulting in positive thoughts you want to share with your audience. However, while this confidence is encouraging, it's important to be honest about your story to achieving your success, providing the audience with your full and transparent journey. They need to know the struggles, losses, and ins-and-outs that you had to encounter in order to get to where you are today. Exemplifying that negative experiences don't necessarily lead to negative outcomes makes your personal struggle extremely relatable to your audience. Don't be afraid to share your setbacks; someone in your audience may be facing issues that they think could destroy them, but hearing about how you overcame your struggles might be their blessing in disguise.

When speaking to an audience of this nature, it is vital that your story is real. It must represent who you are and your journey in life. At points, you will feel vulnerable. Your audience might ask you for more information or for more stories from your past. If your past includes secrets that you do not wish to disclose, do not make up information in place of sharing. Of course, you are not obligated to divulge everything, but do build your story with complete authenticity without hurting your dignity or the dignity of your loved ones.

I highly encourage you to dig more to find your story. You might not think it's impactful, but discovering the message within this story will lead to great success in your mission; sometimes, your story can even be about that moment of discovery.

Discovering your purpose and your story is a major achievement, especially when it comes at later stages in life. It might be so dramatic that you decide to change your routine, your job, or even your spouse to be able to pursue this purpose, proving to be both a powerful and satisfying realization. However, it is crucial to never regret your past; those years made you a warrior in preparation and training. It is your fate that you had to wait longer than others to be able to reach this point of discovery. The timing is part of the purpose. You begin the journey at the right time, while being surrounded by the right people. It might be later than you had hoped, but it's never too late.

Chapter Takeaway

This chapter is the reminder we all need to honor our experiences and stories. Professionals and inspirational storytellers should not shy away from sharing their truth; they owe it to their audience to show up and speak about their journey.

Always remember that the authenticity of your story is what will truly resonate with your audience. This story is linked directly to your purpose in life. The day you know your purpose is the day of your enlightenment, the beginning of your success as a public figure.

Once you find your purpose, look for your audience or clients. They are the ones who have experienced similar circumstances, the ones who want to follow your path. These are the groups that you were born to inspire and motivate. When you connect with your target audience, they will be ready to listen to your story and be vulnerable with you.

If you are a person who believes that your story must be heard, then you should start to tell it as soon as possible. Whether you're an expert in a specific field or you offer another kind of valuable service, you should begin to build your story today. If you believe that you can inspire younger generation to follow in your footsteps and succeed as you did, writing your success story in a timely manner is of the utmost importance. Picking your story will give birth to your personal brand.

Lastly, make sure to be transparent about your story and your expertise. Your audience needs to truly *see* and *hear* you. They need to see more of the "good famous" that could motivate their kids, and they need to understand the value that you are here to offer.

Chapter Activity

If you haven't found your purpose or your message to the world, I happily encourage you to do the following activity. I assure you that it will be a great first step in embarking on your journey.

Ask three friends, three colleagues, and three family members to describe you in three words. Ask them to focus on your skills and highlight your strengths, as opposed to your weaknesses. Sometimes we really need to see ourselves through the lens of others. Explain to them that it is part of a personality test, as you don't want to bias their answers if they know the main objective of the questionnaire.

Once you collect the words, look for commonalities or similar descriptions. Pick three commonalities and try to extract your purpose out of them. Good luck ☺

My Friends' Words:

My Colleagues' Words:

My Family's Words:

I AM A _____ , _____ &
_____

My story will be about:

TWO

Define Your Enemies

"There is only one thing that makes a dream impossible to achieve: the fear of failure."

Paulo Coelho, *The Alchemist*

Now that you already know the story that you will use to manifest your purpose, you may wonder, *why didn't I think about this before? What is stopping me?* Most self-development books ask you to fight the inner voice that stops you. I would encourage you to do the same, and I'll show you how to deal with these inner voices that are stopping your soul from shining.

I used to pray to God and say, "Please God, I want to have an impact. I don't want to leave this life without a meaningful mission. God! You gave me many great things and I am grateful for every single blessing that I have, but please allow me to be one of your tools on this earth to serve and help others. You know what's best, and I ask you for guidance."

I've always wanted to leave a legacy. I knew that I could use my talents to serve the world, but there were some made-up obstacles stopping me from moving forward. And I was the one who made them up! My inner voices deceived me for a long time, hiding the most amazing door that would lead me to my purpose. Some books talk about the subconscious mind and how we need to reprogram it to stop producing negative thoughts. Whether you call it a voice or a subconscious, it is coming from within. This chapter is dedicated to facing your own made-up excuse, what we'll call "the enemy." We create these enemies and allow them to control us. We allow them to lead us into a lazy life, one where we feel complacent in not living our purpose…yet. The truth is that we get complacent at certain times, and we don't want our brain to over-analyze. We feel that it is too hard and requires too much effort to have a purpose. It feels much easier to forget about the whole idea and just keep doing what we're doing. We already have everything we need, right? This is part of the illusion that the enemy wants us to believe.

Below I've listed some of the excuses to try and help you deal with these enemies. At the end of the chapter, I will ask you to be brave and fight your own enemy with a simple exercise. Just remember not to be too hard on yourself; at the end of the day, we are products of societies and environments that shape our perspectives and attitudes. Some of us just need more time and effort to build our rich and purposeful life.

Let's imagine this: you are sitting with some friends or family, and they tell you how much of a talented cook you are, or how you are the world's greatest mom. What would your response be? Would you feel shy? Flattered? Proud? Or would you feel that maybe this talent is your actual tool to live your purpose?

Do you remember the last time you used your talent to educate others, to help others, or even to change the lives of others? God gives us talents and skills so that we can help those who are still in search of their mission. We should think this way. We should believe that each one of us can have an influence and an impact. If you are reading these words and you believe in your talent and your story, then what's stopping you? The truth is, you know what is stopping you. It is the excuse that you tell yourself before you talk about it to others. You get so comfortable with that excuse that you start to see it as your reality. You enjoy helping and educating others around you, but you shy away from reaching out to other people who might need your help.

Before starting to this book, I kept on saying, "I don't know what is stopping me." Everyone who was close to me knew that I was losing many opportunities, but they did not know why until I forced myself to face the truth and to list my excuses. I didn't want to blame anybody or play the victim. I took full responsibility and decided to face my enemies alone. I created them and I can, for sure, make them disappear. I observed my behavior and the words that I used when I asked myself about my purpose. I realized that I often mentioned excuses like, *it's too hard* and *time consuming* or *I don't know how to start, I need someone to help me,* and so on. The reality is that I didn't need the help of anyone to start building my personal brand. All of these excuses were mind blockages that were placed by yours truly. They are enemies of my own success, and no one could defeat them but me.

So now I will tell you about my enemies, and some other excuses that stopped others from showing up and shining bright as brands and as influencers.

Enemy 1 | I don't have time (I have other things to do first)

Out of all enemies, this is the most used excuse. I have used it so many times, but COVID-19 showed me that I was mistaken. Do you remember when we used to say, "If I had more time, I would read all of the most recommended books that I keep on buying and shelving, and I would work on my hobbies"? During the long and arduous days of lockdown, many of us had more free time than we ever had before. Did you *really* use it wisely? How productive were you? Did you reach a major goal? If you did, congratulations, because you are a hero. I was very productive, but I was running away from my purpose. That's another trick that our brain uses against us; now that I have plenty of time, let's do everything I can to distract me from focusing on my purpose. In general, we all bring false priorities to our life just to fill our time. Once our schedules are chock full of activities, we can fool ourselves again by thinking that that we don't have time.

This is exactly what happened to me. I used my time "wisely": I learned how to bake bread, how to color with patience, and how to use the marketing tricks on Instagram. I attended many online workshops and trainings. I got myself so busy and I ran away from the main task that I wanted to complete; writing this book! I came to this realization after about eight months, and this time, I couldn't blame my work or hectic schedule; I had run out of excuses, and I saw my enemies right in front of me. I had no choice but to sit down and fight the fight. All of the past years I was complaining because I didn't have enough time, but when I finally had it, I misused it and tried to get myself busy with other activities.

If lack of time is one of your enemies, you need to learn and commit to using some time management tricks. I know, I know, you've tried this before and it did not work. Well, you have to start again. You have to reach out for a little bit of extra guidance. An expert can be your coach, search for communities to support you, or Google the best ways to force yourself to start building your legacy. The world needs you now more than ever. You deserve to take your role in life. Why wait any longer? You own your time and even if it's only a few minutes a day, you can use it to take the first step.

Think of someone you know who loves to nag you all the time and ask them to push you to start. You need this kind of honest person in your life to hold you accountable and force you to start—and finish—your tasks.

Enemy 2 | I don't know how to do it (it's too complicated)

This is the easiest enemy to defeat. In today's world, you can learn pretty much any and all skills remotely. To start, identify what you are feel you are lacking. Do you lack the marketing skills? Do you need someone to coach you on how to speak publicly? Do you need to build further knowledge in your respective field? Once you know what's missing, the solution is easy. If you feel that you're missing a skill in your field, then you know how to develop your knowledge best. If it is about digital marketing and social media, there are many agencies and coaches who can help you in your journey. Sure, I understand that you might not have the money to invest in marketing agencies.

Chances are that you know someone who loves to create content and is rather savvy when it comes to marketing. If that's the case, asking a young person in your circle of friends or family to help can be a great solution; you'll be amazed at how many of them are willing to help without asking for anything in return. It's important to tap into this person's knowledge and enthusiasm, as they might become your assistant or even consultant in the future. In the meantime, you may even be empowering them to find their own purpose!

All that we learn is going to add to our personality and perspectives in life. Even if you don't use this knowledge at the moment, rest assured that you will use it one day. Do not hesitate to take courses online and to get acquainted with new skills. There are many free or reasonably priced courses on the internet. If you do have the budget, there are plenty of eager experts to hire and who would love to help guide you on your journey.

Enemy 3 | Trying to be famous is degrading

This is a big enemy, especially in conservative cultures. When I started to offer coaching services for professionals who wanted to build their personal brands, I realized that many of them had a negative perspective of fame, often used the word "degrading." This could be specific to my culture in the Middle East, or perhaps it is a general feeling among well-established professionals on a global scale.

In the past, doctors and lawyers would not use advertisements because of the general belief that if they focus on practicing their profession with dignity, people will trust them and continue to ask for their services. However, this same methodology can't be applicable for today's modern landscape. The number of highly-educated, experienced professionals around the world is quickly growing, creating competition to effectively reach more and more clients. Being famous or frequently appearing in the media will not negatively affect your image; the secret is in your message and your content.

Good fame requires smart marketing tactics that will not degrade you, but will rather highlight your strengths through your story and purpose. Fame is not greed, and it is not reserved for Hollywood celebrities. It is for you, as long as you are willing to share your story. People won't think you are too commercial, or you are running after money and fame for the sake of profit. If you use the right message combined with the right media, people will see who you are and how you can help them.

Some professionals have fallen into the trap of building material-istic influence in the media. They are not focusing on their service and purpose especially when they are paid generously to market products of other brands. However, building your brand is not like being a social media influencer. When you are building your personal brand, you are sharing your story with the audience, spreading your message, and connecting with *your* clients, as opposed to social media influ-encers, who use their channels to market and sell the products and services of many companies.

Enemy 4 | It will affect my relationship(s)

I will admit that working on your personal brand requires a signifi-cant amount of time. You will need to manage your schedule to make time for posting on social media, replying to messages, filming videos, and more. Yes, you can hire an agency to manage your website and your social media accounts, but to succeed in your brand, you will have to perform some tasks on your own. Along with being a commit-ment, it takes your relationship with your audience to the next level.

Your partner will have to understand that fame will include them. Always remember that your relationship with family and friends should come first. Begin with baby steps, like crafting simple accounts with simple posts. If you are including your partner in your posts, keep in mind that they will have to approve these steps, as they might have different feelings about appearing in the public. If they feel uncomfortable, try to convince them by taking it really slow, with or without the help of an agency. Let your partner get comfortable with the idea of fame and understand that it will not take you from them; assure them that every issue can be solved if you approach it with wisdom and safety for your loved ones.

When I opened a business account on Instagram, my husband was not very comfortable being included in my content, especially since some of his friends were following my account. He began to get jealous, paying special attention to the pictures I was posting and the outfits I was wearing. At first I was annoyed, but then I understood his point of view. Coming from a very conservative background, he was worried that our friends and family would speak negatively about us. But slowly, as time went on, he started to get relaxed with the idea as my account grew into a professional and work-centric platform. We often take selfies together and I post them as well, so that all my followers can know of him and see how I include him in my virtual life.

After taking these steps, I am able to manage my personal brand without disturbing my relationship with my husband. The most important thing is patience; make a promise to yourself and to your loved ones that your relationships will always come first, and if at any point your work causes harm to those relationships, you will immediately reconsider your actions. This is the beauty of flexibility. Being able to modify your work at any time for the benefit of your health and your relationships brings a level of comfort and understanding to my everyday life. I love my work, but I know how to manage my priorities, and you need to know yours as well. No one knows your life and your partner better than you; you are the only one who knows how to balance being successful at work and being happy at home.

Enemy 5 | Fear

Fear is an enemy that often hides behind pride and comfort. It's difficult to admit that you are afraid; we prefer to mask our feelings with any name but fear. We might say, *I still need to work on my purpose* or *I'm not ready to start my personal brand.* This enemy needs a lot of honesty and maturity.

My clients usually fear two main outcomes: failure and judgment. They never say it out loud, but I recognize it immediately. Some clients are more honest, asking me outright, "What if I fail?" My answer is always the same: nothing will happen. There is no failure in building your personal brand unless you are caught in a criminal or unethical act.

Although there is no failure, there may be a delay. You don't have to be booked for public speaking in your first month. You do not have to have 5,000 followers in the first year. We all have to be patient. While writing this book, I have only 12,000 followers, and it does not bother me, because I know I am building trust. I am not selling lipsticks and bags, but my 12K followers see me as role model. They respect me and respect my opinions, and they come to me looking for motivation. It took me two years to get here, and I am proud of my progress.

Each case is unique depending on your service and the type of audience you appeal to. If you are talking about motherhood, you might gain more followers than a scientist trying to educate people about the power of genetic engineering, simply because there are so many mothers searching for community support. If you've survived cancer, maybe you will be booked for inspirational public speaking events more than a person who started a blog about the art of knitting. Believe in your story and your purpose; your brand will grow eventually, and people will know you and you will be able to serve them at the right time, in the right setting.

Another big fear is judgment. Unfortunately, there has been an increase in online bullying. Anyone can open an account, hiding behind a fake name and hurting others with awful comments. If you really believe in your purpose, you should not be affected by judgments. No one should criticize you or any aspect of your appearance. Even your content is based on your story, and it is no one's place to judge. They were not there with you when you were fighting and struggling. Your purpose is much more important than paying attention to the opinion of others. Focusing on your purpose will show you how to serve, rather than how to please.

Enemy 6 | *I am too old to start now*

This excuse makes me angry, and it's an enemy that I've heard many people mention. I am trying to not use cliches like "it's never too late" or "age is just a number." But those phrases have become cliches precisely because they are so true! When you decide to pursue your purpose and reach out to people, then that is the right time for you to do so. That moment when you start your blog or your YouTube channel *is* the right time! It has nothing to do with your age, your message will be delivered regardless. I assure you that someone who wants to serve others is a person with a young heart. In my opinion, age only adds wisdom and rich experiences to any individual, ideal skills for crafting role models and building personal brands.

I decided to take the first step when I turned 40. It was the age that I felt comfortable with myself, my purpose, and the message I wanted to spread. In my TEDx speech, I was talking about the beauty of "late." For some of us, truly amazing things happen during the later stages of our lives. I believe that God wanted me to have more training in life; He wanted me to be stronger and smarter, and when the time was right, he opened the door by opening my mind and my soul to pursue my purpose. God chose this time for you, and you should respond with gratitude; you still have plenty of time to shine and to inspire others.

Chapter Takeaway

In this chapter, I challenge you to identify the excuses that keep you from pursing your mission in life. You know your purpose, but you think that you are not ready. Yes, we all can be lazy and crave the comfort of doing nothing. Each of us has one or more excuses that we constantly give for not pursuing our purpose. These excuses, or enemies, are mind tricks that we let delay us. Once you identify your enemy, you will be aware of your behavior and try to change it. You will know what to face, and how to face it.

It is always easier to be comfortable, but I assure you that it's so beautiful once you live your purpose and share your story. You will both see and feel a different type of success. You will feel success in every smile you get from your audience, every voice that calls to say, "thank you, you changed my life," every prayer that is sent your way, and every subsequent success story that happened because of your influence. You have to know the enemy with complete honesty. Are you using lack of time as an excuse? Do you lack confidence in your abilities and skills? Are you afraid? These are all crucial questions that you need to address before launching your personal brand.

Chapter Activity

In the table below, list your enemies in the first column. Be honest with yourself. If you have excuses other than the ones listed in this chapter, feel free to write them in the table as well. You need to observe your behavior and the words you use every time you think about your purpose and every time someone asks you what is stopping you.

In the "words" and "feelings" column, write the words that you use to describe this excuse (for example, I am too busy, I do not have time, my life is a mess at the moment, this is not the right time) and list your feelings about it (lazy, comfortable, uncomfortable, etc.)

For the column titled "This is How to Beat It," think about your purpose. Why should you ignore the enemy and continue on your path? What past experiences can you draw from to inspire you and help you fight this particular enemy?

Finally, in the last column, give yourself a concrete action that can help you deal with this enemy (i.e. I will find a software for time management, I will use alarms on my phone, I will focus on my story and purpose for 20 minutes every day, etc.) Here is an example for a dentist.

EXCUSE #1 (ENEMY)	WORDS AND FEELINGS ASSOCIATED WITH THE ENEMY	THIS IS HOW TO BEAT IT	THIS IS WHAT I HAVE TO DO FOR THE NEXT MONTH
• It will degrade my level of professionalism if I become a public figure in the media. • I am a skillful dentist, not an Instagram model.	• It is shameful. • Too commercial; people will not trust me. • I am higher than that. • I am not appreciated in the community.	1. I am passionate about dental health and can educate others about it. 2. I am a skilled dentist who can save my potential patients from amateur and less skilled dentists who are great at selling. 3. My patients deserve to have the best service and I deserve to get the profit. If I become famous from it, I earned that fame.	1. Identify my story and purpose. 2. Identify the way to link my story to the story of my patients. 3. Do some research to know my competition. 4. Take amazing professional photos for my website and professional social media accounts.

Now it's your turn.

EXCUSE (ENEMY)	WORDS AND FEELINGS ASSOCIATED WITH THE ENEMY	HOW TO BEAT IT	THIS IS WHAT I HAVE TO DO FOR THE NEXT MONTH
1.	1.	1.	1.
2.	2.	2.	2.
3.	3.	3.	3.
4.	4.	4.	4.

THREE

Formula Element 1:

ONE THOUGHT, ONE STEP, ONE MASTERPIECE

"Here we go. Another step. Small, bold steps. That's how you change. You must take another step."

Brendon Burchard, *Life's Golden Ticket*

B y now, you have identified the story that will help you to manifest your purpose, and you have beaten your enemies. It is now time to work on the success formula of personal branding; it is time to move forward and take action.

Your first step is your promise and commitment to your purpose. This is when you decide to move and leave laziness behind. You have to do something, anything, that will lead you to your great success.

When I had to work on my dissertation during my PhD program, I spent two months doing absolutely nothing. I was afraid and didn't want to admit that I had created a huge enemy called "fear of failure." Despite the fact that I had the topic and the resources ready, I could not write a word. I preferred to stay in my apartment and watch TV. If anyone asked me about my dissertation, I would say, "I might change the topic, it's not perfect yet." Fearfully, I procrastinated until a friend called me and said, "Samar! Just sit down and write anything.

Just start writing and you will create magic." At that time, I enjoyed working from loud places; I frequented a small Starbucks branch that was close to where I lived. I went to that branch and decided to face my enemy, and my friend was right. I wrote only one paragraph that day, but I was proud and happy to have taken the initial step to get me started and to begin to overcome my fear.

Similarly, when I decided to write this book, it took me two years to take any action. I just needed to start. I eventually did, and I am so glad that I finally pushed myself to write. Even at the times when I stayed up late, almost asleep while writing my words, I was very happy to be working on one of the projects that would help me live my purpose.

In order to start building your brand, all you need is to believe that you are ready to take action. You have defeated your enemies. You know how to stop the excuses that used to slow you down. This is the time to get serious about living your purpose. Never listen to the inner voice that tells you that you are not ready yet—that's an enemy! Just go out, develop your skills and get better at what you do. Fight procrastination: take that communication course online, ask others for help building your website, or open social media accounts. Write one paragraph of your upcoming book, just *one*. At least start to plan your steps. Start somewhere.

Create a Plan | Not all of us are great planners, but we each need a roadmap for our steps or else we get lost and end up deserting our projects. It does not have to be complicated. Many dislike the pressure of commitment, but this is your purpose, and you are the masterpiece! Why would you waste more days and weeks without living the purpose that you were born for?

Never underestimate any simple step that you take in this process. Even something as simple as preparing your favorite cup of coffee to be in a better mood for you to start your plan counts as a step in this beautiful ritual. A graceful butterfly with its thin and fragile wings can eventually create changes in the wind. Find your butterflies and your small actions that will lead you to your personal victory. Yes, the inner thoughts will always be there, and they will try to stop you. And when they do, fight back; keep on visualizing the moments of you living your legacy. The moment you help a parent struggling with their child who has ADHD by teaching them how to deal with this kid. The moment you coach and guide a single mother of five. The moment you start to serve and give. You might face some obstacles and the solution may not be under your control. In this case, you need to learn how to be patient and how to fight the right fight at the right time.

When I was a teenager, I would dream about going to America to pursue my education. I watched American shows, bought American magazines and immersed myself in American culture so that I would understand the lifestyle of the land of my dreams. I used to picture about how I would achieve my goals and the way I would live my daily life in a foreign country. Utilizing the power of my dream, I studied hard to get a full scholarship to study abroad, and I succeeded. After graduating with a high GPA, I applied for the scholarship but unfortunately, my brother refused to allow me to go. He said that I was still too young to go out on my own, and I wasn't ready to live alone. As my legal guardian at that time, I could not disobey him.

I felt that everything had collapsed and that my future had been destroyed—I had a plan and I had followed all the steps, but it did not pan out as I had hoped. It wasn't fair; I knew that I couldn't solve this problem, but I decided that I had lost a battle, not the war. I spent four years studying a major that I did not like, yet I remained on Dean's List every semester. I had used my freedom and my brother's trust wisely. Finally, when I graduated, I had applied for a post-grad-uate scholarship program and was accepted. I was old enough and ready enough to leave. My brother was finally convinced and allowed me to travel.

I was living the time of my life. It took me eight years of planning, but it didn't matter because in the end, I was able to live my dream. I lived every visual thought that I had when I was a teenager. I realized that planning and being patient *can* pave the way for a person to reach their goals.

If living your purpose is not happening now, do not lose your faith. Keep on trying! You can convince others and you can go through all difficulties. Have a plan and trust the journey every step of the way. When you plan the journey, you will be able to celebrate your steps and your achievements. Without the plan, you will live with randomness. Random success moments do not define a journey of an achiever; they can lead to the loss of mission and purpose. Remember to start with a simple plan that you can build upon throughout your journey.

The First Steps of Your Journey | I understand that taking the first step is incredibly difficult. Modern life is so full of distractions; whenever you think about searching for a training course to develop your skills, a compelling advertisement appears, leading you to their website to browse their online products. Once you tell yourself that it's time to open a social media account, you receive a message on WhatsApp and get caught up in conversation. Days go by and you drift further and further away from living your legacy. Seize the moment; it's time to get committed and be serious. People who need you are waiting to see your shine.

One of the reasons I wanted to write this book was to help others to start and move forward. To do this, I began to think about ways to encourage my readers to start their journey. I prepared some basic parameters based on my journey that will eventually lead you to live your purpose. The following guidelines are crucial to push you toward achieving your goal.

Plan Your Journey | Randomness will lead to loss. When you are committed to serve, you need to start planning. It does not have to be a formal plan with SMART (specific, measurable, attainable, relevant, time-based) goals just yet; all you need is to write down, or even draw, your main objectives or your most-needed actions. Once you identify the story that you are going to share with your audience, you need to know how to link it to your purpose and plan for building your personal brand.

Let's say you were able to recover from a severe trauma with the help of yoga, leading you to become an expert. You believe that there are many people who are suffering mentally and emotionally, just as you had. You know that you can help them and show them the path for peace of soul and mind. You know that it's time to build your personal brand. What could be the best plan? Most likely, you'll need to do some research first to understand types of traumas and what people go through based on scientific facts. You will also want to identify the target market. Moreover, you have to find your unique message. Which story you will use and how you will use it? You need an objective, your target market, your unique message, and a reason for the audience to connect with you.

Determine Your Necessary Resources | Each step will require some resources. You might need to read books, watch documentaries, or even survey people to learn about their needs. Knowing the needs will help you identify the way your message will relate to them. Also, you might need to invest in your own education to be ready. Knowing the actions will make the journey easier and more realistic. It is no longer a dream or a vision, it is your daily reality and your lifestyle.

Celebrate Every Step | It is okay to feel happy and excited for the simplest reason. If you found an article that will help in your journey, enjoy the feeling and celebrate. I love chocolate, so I reward myself with dark chocolate to celebrate small wins. If I achieve a big goal, I pamper myself with something else. Go ahead and reward yourself for small victories! This will help you stay motivated. Book a massage session or treat yourself to lunch or dinner at your favorite restaurant after spending days on the computer finishing a task. Every time you finish a task, you are a step closer to living your purpose. You are answering the call of the universe. You are the only one who can pace this process, depending on your abilities, your priorities, and your family circumstances. Don't rush things just because you are excited. Remember that slow cooking gives you the most delicious meals.

· · ·

Make It a Habit | My friends always ask me, "How do you keep going to the gym with such a busy schedule? Don't you get tired of it?" My answer is, "I made it a habit." I know that each and every day, I have to pray, sleep, eat, drink, work, take care of others, and exercise. The trick is to force yourself to do it for a couple of weeks, and if you keep up with it, it quickly becomes a habit. Instead of feeling forced into it or bored, this habitual routine is a blessing and becomes a wonderful part of your day. If you keep working on your plan and toward achieving your goals, it will even become a joyful habit. It is your purpose and your legacy, and you will always be proud of every step. Even if you have a lot of success, or become an influencer and a role model, you will still need to keep this habit of seeking growth. Living your purpose is an extended yet beautiful process that is always evolving. Serving and helping others will continue to be part of your day, but you'll need to keep on developing your knowledge and skills to be able to continue serving.

Ask For Help When You Need It—and You Will Need It | When starting off, you most likely won't have to have every skill needed to successfully complete your journey. To help you get there, you will probably need some help.

There is nothing wrong with asking for help; in fact, it's a sign of strong leadership. For example, you don't have to be an expert in marketing to build your personal brand. There are multiple agencies and boutique businesses that can help. By using them as tools, they will help you as you focus on creating the content that fits your audience. Delegation is great as well. Freelancers are happy to work with you on certain tasks at a relatively low expense. If your nephew knows how to build professional websites, try asking him to help build one for you. Ask your daughter to be your communication manager and help with phone calls and emails. Empower the youth in your community and allow them to feel important and needed, ultimately encouraging them to become the heroes for tomorrow.

Following these guidelines will hopefully start your journey, step-by-step, towards living your purpose, from choosing your story to planning your personal brand.

Chapter Takeaway

In this chapter, you learned about the first element of my personal branding formula. I aimed at encouraging you to take action and start pursuing your purpose, starting with baby steps. It may be difficult, but if you follow these guidelines, you will be able to launch your personal brand, hopefully in a couple of months. Always remember that you must believe in your purpose, pick your story, and defeat your enemies in order to achieve your goals. You are working on a master-piece, which is you! Taking time to understand how to manifest your purpose translates into planning; with a clear plan, you can divide your major milestones into small steps. These small steps or tasks that are actionable on a daily or weekly basis will allow you to celebrate small successes, preparing for your big moment as a role model, influencer, or motivator. For the first element of the formula, these guidelines are meant to help you start planning your steps, identify the actions associated with each step, celebrate the completion of every action, make your journey a joyful habit, and finally, ask for help whenever you need it. In the next section you will find a table that can be attached or included in your planner. It might inspire you to start planning. Don't hesitate, just start.

Chapter Activity

Once you are ready with your story, it's time to start moving forward. Remember, everything should move according to your circumstances. There is no need to rush, but you should take consistent actions and try not to procrastinate. Use your monthly planner or the calendar on your phone to set a schedule for your work. Make it fun and full of celebration. This is you, the masterpiece—it should represent your personality and what you want to give back to the universe. It is not a boring work schedule; rather, it is your map to reach success. If you see this schedule as a hefty commitment, then it's not the right time for you to start. You need to be excited and happy about the process; you should look forward to it because it is moving you forward as well. Here is an example:

MONTH 1: THE MONTH OF RESEARCH

WEEK/DATE	OBJECTIVE	TASKS	WHO CAN HELP ME?	IS IT DONE?
Week 1	I need to know who is offering the same service to my audience (competition)	• Research social media accounts • Identify 3 strong competitors	Cousin "K"	😎
Week 2	I need to list 10 ideas for my blog's articles	• Write a summary for each topic until I finalize the list	I have to do it myself	😐

Try to do this planning for a maximum of three months. You can write the details of each task for every day, and you can use your planner or digital calendar to schedule one or two specific days a week to dedicate time to each task. Now it's your turn.

MONTH # _____ TITLE:_____

WEEK/DATE	OBJECTIVE	TASKS	WHO CAN HELP ME?	IS IT DONE?
Week 1				
Week 2				
Week 3				
Week 4				

FOUR

Formula Element 2:

CREATION ABOVE COMPETITION: YOU ARE HERE TO
SERVE

"We'd achieve more if we chase the dream instead of the competition."

Simon Sinek

"Competition is healthy" is a phrase you've probably heard many times before. While there is some truth to that old cliche, it's only actually healthy if you allow it to be. When it comes to building your personal brand, your main goal is to serve people. If you know about others with the same mission, you should be happy that they're doing similar work, not angry. Don't fall into the trap of fear of competition. There will be hundreds of people who share the same purpose as you, so focus on what *you* have to offer. Each person is unique in the value that they provide to an audience; *everyone* has a story to tell. The message might be the same, but your style, story, and content will make you stand out. Believe in what you are creating without being distracted by the competition. Even if you are a professional who is hoping to get more clients through the success of your personal brand, try to think beyond profit. Remember, the purpose of this book is to help you get ready for a personal brand that will turn you into a "good famous" role model who motivates younger generations. You will make a profit eventually, and it will be based on value, not on a war with your competition.

To be able to see competition as a healthy practice, you need to identify the mental traps you should avoid, and defeat, during your journey. These thoughts will come to you, and you need to keep encouraging yourself to face them with the truth: you are a masterpiece, and your story is unique. Your special audience is waiting for you to shine; you won't disappoint them or keep them waiting. When you avoid these mental traps, the value you offer will successfully connect you with the audience.

Mental Trap 1 | There are many other successful people with the same story and the same mission. I will not make a difference.

Do you know for sure that your story will not make a difference? Would you try to inspire even one person, or would you rather forget about your purpose and your legacy? That one person is a start; they will influence their family and friends, and you will see the amazing ripple effect that one person can create. As a teacher in the modern age, I face challenges when working with my students. Some are ambitious and love to learn, but most come to class primarily focused on getting a passing grade. It can be depressing and discouraging at times, and when I feel down, I remind myself that I can influence one student at a time. If I can teach one student something beneficial to help them in the future, then I succeeded in my mission. Each one of you reading this book will be able to influence thousands of people around the world—just by believing in your purpose.

Mental Trap 2 | Oh my God, they are so good and full of energy, I can't be like them.

Who said you have to be like them? Why do you think that you have to walk the same steps? Once you share your story with complete honesty, the audience will connect with you and see your value. They will not compare you to your competition. If they do, it will be based on the marketing tactics that you used, not based on your story. In fact, the people you are comparing yourself to are so good because they have what we call a "learning curve." They started ahead of you; they developed and utilized their skills very well and in time, you will be as good as they are, or even better. Your confidence will grow each day—as will your energy and excitement—as you receive messages from all the people you've inspired. Comparing yourself to someone who is far ahead of you isn't fair. You didn't see them when they got their start, what they felt and what skills they lacked. The focus should be on you and how to develop your skills, day by day. As a journey that has its ups and downs, it requires your personal investment for unbelievably rewarding results.

Mental Trap 3 | *I am too old (or young), who will listen to me?*

Being too old or too young does not mean that you don't have value. The energy that you need will not come from your age, but rather from the light inside your soul and the energy of your story. People will become attracted to you because they see honesty and authenticity in your eyes. Use your age in its most genuine form, as an advantage. If you are an older and more experienced individual, connections with the younger generation will happen, because they will see their future in you. They will learn about the journey of life from you. If you are young with an impactful story, all generations will respect your courage and honesty. Modernly representing your story and teachings will help to successfully convey your message.

Mental Trap 4 | *They look amazing, and I don't.*

Love yourself the way you are, without fear of judgment. Some-times it feels like we are living in a very materialistic and shallow world, but always remember that if you want to inspire, you will only succeed if you wear your confidence. No need for fancy clothes or makeup to deliver your message. Yes, appearance is a factor, but your soul is the main influencer. The fear of judgment is a real enemy—fight it hard. People need to connect with your story, not your looks.

After gaining a social media audience of a couple thousand followers, I started to pay more attention to my sense of fashion. I followed a few social media accounts that give great fashion advice. Now I'm able to pick the right outfits that suit my message and my personality. I am doing the minimum not because of competition, but because it's part of my message and image. I never copy my competition; I just follow what suits me.

There are no standards for beauty. You are beautiful already, just because you want to help. Don't you find kind people very beautiful? There is something about them that attracts others, regardless of their looks. They simply shine with a sense of comfort and inner beauty.

Once you are aware of these traps, hopefully, you will not fall into them. Keep the focus on your purpose and creating the personal brand that is going to allow you to serve. What you create is what's going to live forever; your influence, articles, books, videos, or podcasts will be available for others to get inspired and motivated. This is not to say that you should completely ignore the competition; but rather, learn to deal with the concept of competition in a constructive way. We will touch on these in further chapters, but to help, I have prepared the following recommendations to aid you in your journey.

1. Know that competitors will always exist and grow in number

The first thing to do is to accept the fact that you are not the only person who is trying to serve and live their purpose. It's quite amazing to see how many people are sharing your same intention! They should not be the source of fear. They are a confirmation that what you are doing is great and there is a need for this kind of service.

Imagine you're a dentist who is trying to educate parents on how to raise their kids with full awareness of the importance of dental care. There are many other dentists who are trying to reach the same goal—but there is space for all of you, because this work is important and necessary. All of you are contributing to the healthy futures of the new generations, and all of you are doing an amazing job. All you have to do is differentiate yourself with the content that you create and the story you share with the audience.

2. Focus on five competitors, at max

When I was a kid, my father and I watched a movie about a historical hero in the Muslim world. I was amazed by the character's ability to think strategically about his enemy's tactics and to predict their next move. My father explained that in war, you need to think about your enemy as if you are in love with them. When you become a fan, you will know their every move. You will know how they think and what they do. When you hate the enemy, you are blinded by anger and even fear.

Become a fan of three to five competitors in your field, ones that you view as successful. Watch what they do, what they post on social media, and how they communicate with their audience. Don't copy what they are doing but see what you can learn them. Seeing their achievements and mistakes will not only save you time and effort but will also help you build a plan on how you will shine and differentiate yourself.

3. There has to be space for you to compete

In marketing, this space is called a competitive advantage, but when building a personal brand, I will call it influence advantage. Your influence is unique; you will use your own story to represent your thoughts and emotions. Even if there are many people sharing the exact same message as you, you will be different in the way you use your personal story. Whether you're a parent, a cancer survivor, an artist, or simply a human who has faced special circumstances, all you have to do is find your point of differentiation. When you open your heart and start to share your story, you will realize the uniqueness of your purpose.

4. Consider cooperation

I highly recommend building a network with others who share your same purpose. You will connect on similar experiences, tips and tricks for your journey and content. At the end of the day, you are all trying to inspire and help a similar audience. Why not do it together? Work on a documentary, a podcast, or a guide to benefit the audience. As long as you see what you are doing as a service to the universe, then collectively cooperating with your competition will be the most logical way to spread the message and to reach a broader audience. You will be amazed by the responses of your competitors; most will greet you with joy and support. They might even become your allies or future collaborative partners. Have good intentions and all of the good outcomes will come to you.

Chapter Takeaway

This chapter represents the second element of my success formula and the main aspect of your personal brand, otherwise known as your uniqueness. The whole idea of building your personal brand is to use it as a vehicle to reach people who need to hear your story. We talked about competitors—or fellow motivators—that will always appear and challenge you. It is absolutely okay to have them on your journey, because they will push you to grow, and they will confirm your purpose. Competitors will always be there, and you will need to develop the talent of turning their challenge into a window for growth.

We also touched on negative thoughts. Your brand is your positive contribution to the world, so why start it with negative comparative thoughts? We get negative thoughts all the time, but we should never surrender to them. We need to turn them into opportunities for reality change. This chapter included some ways to think about your negative thoughts, both logically and effectively.

Chapter Activity

This chapter will include two activities: the first will build your awareness of mental traps, while the second will set you up to learn from your competitors.

In the first activity, you will identify and acknowledge the mental traps that appear and determine what you will say to yourself to counter their effects. Personalize this for yourself; feel free to add any negative thoughts that come to you on your own.

Mental Trap: They are so good at what they do, I am not.

I tell myself: It's okay, I'm developing my skills and training to be as good as they are. I will perfect this.

Now it's your turn.

Mental Trap: _____

I tell myself: _____

Mental Trap: _____

I tell myself: _____

Mental Trap: _____

I tell myself: _____

Mental Trap: _____

I tell myself: _____

Mental Trap: _____

I tell myself: _____

Mental Trap: _____

I tell myself: _____

Mental Trap: _____

I tell myself: _____

Keep practicing this until you no longer see this trap or get this negative thought. Be patient and take your time until you see your victory.

For the second activity, watch your top competitors closely. Start with three competitors whose purpose is very similar to yours. Identify what makes you similar and what differentiates you from them. To motivate yourself, look at their points of strength—what are they great at? This should inspire you to develop your own skills.

In chapters to come, we will discuss the benefits of potential future collaboration opportunities as part of your plan for growing your personal brand.

COMPETITOR'S NAME	THEIR BEST PRACTICES/TRAITS	SIMILARITIES IN THE MESSAGE OR PURPOSE	SOURCES OF YOUR UNIQUENESS	OPPORTUNITY FOR FUTURE COLLABORATION
Example: XXX YYY	• They have creative production for their videos on social media.	• They are experts in educating parents with kids with special needs.	• I am a parent of 2 kids with special needs who already graduated from college. • My story is unique.	• Host them on my podcast show. • Create educational videos together.

FIVE

Formula Element 3:

YOUR STORY IS YOUR BRAND

"Yes, in all my research, the greatest leaders looked inward and were able to tell a good story with authenticity and passion."

Deepak Chopra

Now that we have our story and our content, how do we turn that into a brand that can be communicated professionally? Usually my students ask me, "How could a person become a brand?" The brand is like an ID card—whether it's ID for a company, a non-profit entity, or a person, that ID card represents you and what you are doing. The design of this ID card will differ based on your target market and the image you want to portray. The products and services offered are essential parts of the brand. But when the brand is a person, that person becomes the main product. Of course, we are not selling the person, but we are instead offering their services and thoughts.

One could ask "Why can't I just post any picture and start writing whatever I want to write?" It's not that simple. We all need to remember to respect the audience and the message that represents our purpose. When you distinguish yourself with the right communication tools, you are showing respect and care to your audience. At the same time, you're allowing yourself to deliver the message in a straightforward way. You are not after random acts and superficial influence; you want to leave an impact and inspire others. Your impact needs your signature. When you are building your personal brand, you are not selling; you are calling for others to listen to your message. I was always active on social media, consistently posting pictures and motivating quotes. But I wasn't able to reach my audience until I decided to apply the concept of branding to my communication strategy. It organized my messages and it made my communication look more professional, reaching people way beyond my geographical location.

As previously mentioned, you need to start with a story in order to live your purpose and leave a legacy in this world. The audience can feel the emotional connection through the stories that we share. They need to know that we understand what they are going through or have already gone through. Only then will they give us their attention and respect. If you stay authentic and honest, they will continue to trust and respect you. They will start to see you as the hero they want to be. The way you tell the story is going to establish your brand. People will know you through this story, and they will connect with you because of this story.

When choosing a story, there are certain aspects that need to be considered. In addition to authenticity, you also need to form your unique story in a way that will lead to the success of your brand, leading you to influence and motivate your followers. To do so, your story should serve four main functions:

1. Attract the audience through your character and emotions
2. Motivate the audience to reach the desired outcomes
3. Inspire the audience for growth
4. Turn the audience into clients (if applicable).

To complete those functions, each personal story should include the following:

· · ·

Your Character | People will see themselves in your character, so it's extremely important to be very intentional about the way you represent this character in the story. Make sure to represent a normal, relatable person—don't be arrogant nor frail when telling your story. You will act as a leader for your audience, holding their hand during their journey. Be the guide they trust and the role model they look up to.

The Emotions | Your story will include many deeply-felt emotions, both positive and negative. If your story conveys and shows vulnerability and authenticity, your audience will feel those same emotions. Establishing emotional connections and references is going to build a bond with your audience, grow your personal brand and incite loyalty amongst your followers. Being vulnerable and standing in your truth will allow others to feel connected to you, showing them that they are not alone—if you could persevere through those difficult emotions, so can they.

The Exact Problem or Situation | The story should represent a problem or a situation that led you to become the person you are—the exact situation that inspired you to build your brand. A common mistake people make is talking about their emotions without focusing on the most important moment—the moment they knew their life was changing because of a specific reason or event. This problem or situation is what will really attract the audience to your brand, as many individuals will be able to relate to the same problems or similar situations. You can keep on talking about the hardships of, say, being a parent of a child with special needs, and people will connect with your message, but your audience needs to know how you managed this situation and what changed your life.

The Outcome and The Solution | Your story should include the important milestones and wins that you have experienced to inspire your audience. They want to see the exit from that critical situation, the taste of success, the solution to the problem and the overcoming of loss. The happy ending, or at least the hope to reach it, is what keeps the audience in your story. If you haven't found the solution yet, taking your audience on your daily journey as you seek that resolution is both hopeful and encouraging. Someone who is fighting cancer might want to show the world his positive outlook and encourage other patients—this, by itself, is part of your inspiring story and solution.

How to Grow from There | There is no end to your happiness and achievements. Showing your audience that the sweet taste of success could last, and grow, is inspiring. Your continuous success and growth will push them to work harder and to grow as well. What happens after winning the race? What will you do after beating cancer? How will you grow after being a successful lawyer? People need to be challenged and pushed for the next step. Even if you are just starting your journey, you can use modern communication tools such as social media to show your growth and progress. Daily posts that show progression in your life and your journey can encourage your followers to move forward as well.

Call To Action *(if applicable)* | Your story's outcome is the best start to turn your audience into clients. When people see that your solution worked for you (and maybe for others), they would want to seek help from you. They will eventually ask for professional advice or coaching services as they too are hungry for the solution. The more your story relates to the audience, the bigger the chance that they'll become your clients. The excitement of success and the continuous encouragement to pursue life goals will ignite their passion. There is no harm in offering them a free coaching sessions or a discounted training course; you want them to have a taste of what you can offer them. Just make sure that it doesn't feel like you're trying to sell all the time. Drop the offer as a way to help and support.

You talked about your story and victory, and the audience is excited and encouraged to change their realities, but you need to show them the next step to keep up your momentum. Give them a chance to commit to their success by calling them to action.

Now that you have the story that will represent your brand, you need to pay attention to the other ingredients of this beautiful dish. While having a strong story and being unique is important, it's not enough to successfully convey your message.

Picture your personal brand as a piece of steak. The juicy meat is the story you are going to share with the audience. But who eats a piece of meat without anything else served alongside it? You need to add some seasoning, sauces, potatoes, vegetables, bread, or any other side dish. You can have the best story in the world, but it will not have a real impact unless you communicate it the right way, taking into consideration some of these other essential aspects that will guarantee your success:

The Audience | Knowing your audience is the first step to finding the best way to communicate your story. When you know them, you will know what they are going through and the emotions that they are having. You will know how to communicate your message because you will understand their language and use the right words with them. It will make you more sensitive to what discourages them and what ignites their energy. Investing in studying your audience is a requirement for your success. You might want to study the audience of your competition or collect some secondary data from articles and journals that discussed similar stories and similar messages to the ones you have.

Your Image | Whether it's your portrait or professional profile picture, this image has to be inspired by your character in the story. Your image is a visual representation of your personality, level of education, style, traits, and skills. Do you want your audience to see you as a happy person? Are you a classic person? Are you in love with life? Are you a family man? Are you a highly educated and cultured individual? All of these aspects will affect your brand. Pick the right colors, outfits, photos, and style of writing—and enlist the help you need in order to do this, if necessary. Everything you do or say needs to match that image you show. You can't tell your audience to always be happy and love life if your professional photo is sad or overly serious. You can't tell the audience that you're an average, relatable person with a standard education and then use sophisticated, potentially inaccessible language in your writing.

If you ready with your story, know your audience, and have identified your desired image, you have all the ingredients to prepare your steak, but you still need to season and then cook it. Cooking the dish, or introducing your personal brand, requires the flames of marketing and the seasoning of your brand's design. The next chapter will discuss this process and provide you with a guide for the main aspects of marketing before introducing your personal brand. While this is not a branding book per se, you will get an introduction to the main idea of the branding and marketing processes. This will prepare you to select the right agency or freelancer to help you design the creative aspects of your brand.

This may be a lot of information at once, but it's not meant to overwhelm you. The truth is that you can start with what you already have, what you will always have—just be yourself and tell your story. Don't pay attention to the aesthetic aspects or the perfection of the language just yet; that can come later. Follow this guide step by step, and you will find it to be so easy to write your own story in a simple way that will attract the right audience.

Chapter Takeaway

The concept of personal branding can still be confusing for many individuals looking to build themselves in a professional way. Some people cannot digest the idea of turning a person into a brand, thinking that branding is only beneficial for celebrities and influencers on social media. But in truth, personal branding is the best way to organize the communication between professionals and their audiences. With the increase of globalization and the need for public speakers and motivating mentors, personal branding has started to serve new target markets. Your personal brand is like your ID card that will be used in public to identify you and what you have to offer.

This chapter discussed the importance of personal branding and how to get prepared, outlining the main role that your story will play in making your brand successful. I also touched on the main steps to building your personal brand, including identifying your target audience, deciding on your story's public image, and focusing on the main aspects of the story. I compared the process of developing your personal brand to preparing a delicious steak dinner. Having a piece of meat by itself is pretty boring, but once you add some seasoning and side dishes, you truly have a full and happy meal.

Chapter Activity

Let's work on your personal brand, using this template to practice.

Your name: _____

Your target audience *(Include details such as age, gender, location, lifestyle, the relevant problem or issue, or any other important characteristics)*:

_____

A brief synopsis of your story (approximately two paragraphs)

Note: Think about the situation that shaped your journey that your audience will relate to, how you handled it in the past, how are you dealing with it now, what is the best solution or recommendation, what outcome they can expect, and how to get encouraged to grow.

_____
_____
_____
_____
_____

How do you want people to see you (describe the image you want to project)?

_____

Prepare the main ingredients for your dish and join me in the next chapter for some recommendations on how to cook it.

SIX

Formula Element 4:

MARKETING IS YOUR FRIEND: GET TO KNOW IT WELL

"Marketing is the creative use of truth."

Phillip Kotler

Now that you have the tools to build your personal brand, it's time to start thinking about communication. Your story and message both need to reach the audience, and you want to find the best available methods to spread your message.

In an earlier chapter, I described one of the mental enemies which makes you think that marketing can degrade your business and level of professionalism; an accusation that marketers continue to face. At the root of this issue, some people believe that marketing is all about lying and deceiving clients, degrading the industry's many professionals.

It's not the intention of this book to defend marketing, but it is necessary in building your personal brand to think about marketing in today's modern age. Remember this: "As long as there is competition, there is a need for marketing." In other words, as long as you have a message, you need marketing to deliver it. As a person who wants to become a brand, you need to use the tools of marketing. You are not a company that is going to sell products to satisfy specific needs. Instead, you are a great influencer who wants to impact people's lives.

I have met many amazing professionals who have potential to make a great impact on society, but they don't know how to reach the public. Sometimes they try, but without the right tools they end up hurting their image and degrading their professionalism. If I convince them that marketing is good for them, they usually think that it's too easy, that they can do it themselves—another misunderstanding of the value of marketing by underestimating the profession. Even some entrepreneurs and business owners think that marketing is easy and that they can master it by reading a book or taking a course online.

However, marketing is a huge field that includes many subfields. It's both an art and science that can lead a business to major success. Marketing is the connector between a brand and the public, turning potential clients into actual ones. It's the field of creativity and strategic impact. As a professional or a person with a motivating story, you don't need to study marketing. It's not your job to design the brand, or the website, or even create advertisements. If you already have some experience in this field, that's great—you're ready to start. If you simply want to deliver your message, don't bother yourself with learning the secrets of marketing. For your own sake, *think* before starting your brand based on a free online course or video; hire a professional instead.

Your purpose deserves to be treated with care and professionalism, and your story deserves to be told the right way. As a role model, you deserve to give back to society with dignity and respect. I know some doctors who decided to use social media to show their influence. Unfortunately, some of these professionals were posting pictures about fashion and travel and trying to communicate their message using words that were not accessible to the average person. They ended up being fashion influencers instead of impactful, medical role models for future generations. This is what happens when you lose your main goal and focus on the easy, profitable results. These professionals may make more money and they might quit their profession anyway—but what happened to their purpose? Is it really their purpose to tell people to purchase a fancy car or travel to a certain destination?

When you are working with experts on building your personal brand, you only need to understand a few principles of marketing to be able to describe what you're looking for. That's why it was important to add this chapter to my book—to offer some guidelines for my readers to understand the basics of marketing. As an added bonus, knowing the basics will help you manage some of your content on your own in the future. Any details or designs should be created by someone else. If you're a professional such as a doctor or an engineer, you don't want to spend too much time designing a post or editing a video—this is time taken away from your true purpose. Even on a limited budget, asking for help from friends and family will lead you to a person with experience that could assist you in marketing your brand. Alternatively, you can use simple mobile applications that can help you start posting with free designs. You don't have to start with an extremely professional brand that screams sophistication. It's a journey, and you're going to evolve while living your purpose. You'll have many opportunities to enhance your personal brand in the future; stressing yourself with too many details is going to pull you away from the main purpose. Focusing on your message and audience will eventually help you reach your goals.

As this is not a marketing textbook, I will introduce you to some basic ideas to prepare your brand from a marketing perspective. There are certain fundamentals that you need to keep in mind, especially when you are seeking help from a marketing agency.

You and Your Image | I keep on repeating the word "image" because that's what will resonate in the mind of your audience. You need to think about the idea of "you" and what you stand for. Do you want your image to be "the experienced entrepreneur," "the rescuer of stray animals," "the achiever fighting disability," or maybe "the teacher who inspires first graders?" Depending on your purpose, there here are many meaningful images that you can create for yourself. How do you want your audience to see and think of you? This will be reflected in all of the remaining fundamentals. It will also affect your appearance, the way you will share your story, the outfits and accessories you pick, and the tone of the content that you will use. If you pick the wrong image or behave in a way that contradicts your purpose , you will minimize your brand's chances for success. Would a mother showing sadness and desperation motivate you as a new mother? Would a person making rude jokes represent a successful professional?

Think about the people who have inspired you. You'll remember that they always lived in a certain way and showed positive emotions. If your purpose is to motivate and inspire today's youth, be mindful when talking about a personal trauma—while that may be part of your story, the takeaway message needs to be one of hope. You want to show them that there is always growth and new possibilities. That's not to say that you should be inauthentic or use exaggerated positivity to attract an audience; on the contrary, it's important to be yourself and to be in sync with your purpose. Just be careful that sometimes being yourself may override the message you want to deliver. You must write this image on a piece of paper and look at it every day. It will motivate you to create the right content and to behave according to your purpose and your story.

The Audience You Want to Reach | Identifying your audience is extremely important—not only should you know their overarching demographics, but you should also study their behavior and lifestyle. The first and most important characteristic of your audience is that they are looking for a solution to a situation that is similar to the problem conveyed by your story—this is your point of connection. Your audience shares your same pain and struggle; they will feel your emotions when they listen to your story. The second step is identifying your audience's behavior when it comes to using media preferences and their ways of spending free time—you need to understand their lifestyle. Do they spend long hours on social media platforms? Do they love to watch TV? Are they highly educated? Do they like to read? Are they physically active? These answers, along with other details, will help you attract the attention of your audience; you will be able to tailor your message in a way that it is well-suited for your audience.

. . .

Your Message | Why do you want to have a personal brand? Why would your audience connect with you? Answer these two questions in one or two sentences and reflect on them. This is your commitment and promise to your audience. Your intentions will be focused on delivering this message, and it should come with an outcome.

Let's use the following message as an example, "My mission is to empower the youth and coach them to develop their skills so they will have better career opportunities in the future." This sentence can be broken out in three parts: 1. the audience, 2. the message, and 3. the outcome you want them to have. Your message will be rooted in your story, and that story will explain your purpose. It's then a matter of creativity to be able to deliver this message with specific content. Even if you are just starting, remember your message so that you will never drift away from it and confuse your audience. In the example above, the message is about youth empowerment, and it should appear in all of the produced content. The audience should be mostly young people looking to you—the person with the solution--to support or lead them to the outcome they are looking for. Once your brand is well-established and you have a working marketing team, they will know how to utilize words and pictures in the best way to serve your purpose.

The Media Selection | Knowing the media channels that you will use to effectively and efficiently communicate with your audience will accelerate the success of your brand, as well as help you develop content that suits those media channels. You will know how to make your content more appealing based on the characteristics of the media channel. For example, if you know that your audience spends many hours on YouTube, you should create longer videos or webinars. Or, if your audience is into visual social media apps like Instagram or Snapchat, you might want to focus on quick images and shorter videos. If your audience has a large community on Twitter, your content should focus on delivering your message in one or two short sentences at a time. If your audience loves to watch TV, television appearances and interviews will be essential. Each type of media has its advantages and disadvantages. Some come at a higher cost than others or might take more coordination between you and outside parties like public relation agencies. Pick media that is both suitable for you and your budget and, above all, preferred by your audience.

Keeping these fundamental elements in mind and educating yourself about marketing will enable you to imagine your brand and how you're going to communicate with your audience. Even if you're starting without any experience, you will still be able to have an impact because you are focused on your purpose and your audience.

Chapter Takeaway

This chapter is part of the preparation of your personal brand. You might have a great story and impactful message, but if you don't know how to communicate them, your personal brand will not succeed.

Many professionals have come to me for advice after spending a lot of money on marketing agencies without any significant success. Those professionals didn't have a vision for their own personal brand; they just went to an agency and paid the money. While they were happy with the professional photos and the website, lacking knowledge about the fundamental issues in marketing made it impossible for them to manage their brand.

Another reason for a lack in success is that marketing a person is much more difficult than marketing a product, like a burger or an online course. When you're marketing a person, that person has to do the majority of the work and the appearances, as they are the product. It's essential that someone who is responsible for delivering a social message knows the basics of marketing. Because of that, I found the addition of this chapter necessary so that readers can effectively educate themselves or any agency that they are working with on how to prepare for their personal brand.

Remember that your image is essential to starting a personal brand. How do you want people to see and think of you? Your image will create the role model you want to become. It will always remind you of what to say and how to behave. It's your identity in the eyes of the audience. Knowing your image must go hand-in-hand with knowing your audience. If you can, draw a picture of your ideal audience. Imagine their emotions and their pains and identify what you have in common with them so that you can more closely tailor your content, as all of your marketing activities will be directed at them. At the end of the day, you started this brand to inspire them, and they deserved to be understood.

When you understand your audience, you will be able to create the right message. This message is what you are going to convey every time you tell your story; it's what made you start your brand in the first place.

Your personal brand needs to offer a solution or some guidelines to your audience based on your experience—it's of no use to your audience if it's only about your achievements. Your audience should be the hero of the story, and inspiring them comes with showing the finish line and the check mark. That's why you need to have a focus on the outcomes.

Lastly, choosing the right media outlet is what is going to allow you to reach your audience quickly and efficiently. The media should match your skills and your budget, but at the same time, you should pick the most preferred media by your audience. Digesting this information is going to majorly reduce the confusion when you decide to start your personal brand, either by yourself or with the help of a specialized agency.

Chapter Activity

Keep this worksheet with you and put it in a place where you will see it every day. If you hire a marketing agency, make sure to take this worksheet with you. It will guide them on the main elements of marketing your personal brand.

1. I am a: *(a sentence to describe your image and how the audience should think of you. Maybe elaborate on what you wrote in the previous chapter)*

_____

_____

2. This is how I imagine my professional picture should look (looks, outfit, style, face features):

_____

_____

3. These are the emotions I want my audience to feel when I communicate with them:

_____

_____

4. My audience includes: *(detailed description of your audience)*

_____

_____

5. My message is:

_____

_____

6. The outcomes I want my audience to experience are:

_____

_____

7. The media outlets I should focus on are:

_____

_____

SEVEN

Formula Element 5:

TIME TO WORK ON YOURSELF AND GET READY TO SHINE

"Why live an ordinary life, when you can live an extraordinary one."

Tony Robbins

Y ou've probably heard every motivational speaker expounding on the importance of being fit and taking care of your mental and physical health. This message is of the utmost importance! No matter what your message is, attention to your health should be part of your daily process. Even if you're fighting a chronic disease, your brand should inspire others and push them to fight harder. They need to see the result of the fight through your story and brand. When they see you improving, they will be motivated to take care of their own health, and they will wait for your positive energy every day.

There is a lovely lady in my country Kuwait who is fighting cancer and trying to educate others about her disease. She can barely breathe, but even so, every time she films a video she is in full makeup. She uses makeup as a tool to tell others, "I can still feel good and love life, and I am getting better." She deserves to look great despite her illness; this is a form of self-care. The same goes for professionals and public figures; if you are a doctor and you want patients to come to your clinic, you have to show them that you're healthy with the way you look and move. They will know that you are mentally healthy due to your communication style and logical thinking. Who wants to hire a messy looking lawyer? Who would go to a doctor who is a heavy smoker that coughs all the time? Who would be motivated by a depressed individual with very weak energy and obvious grudges? When you're healthy, you have a clear mind to generate the message you were born to deliver.

I'm not an expert in the medical field, and I'm not copying what other authors are saying. I am a woman who suffered from many health issues that I wasn't even aware of at the time. In 2014, a year after getting married to my amazing husband, I started to feel that there was something wrong with me. I have always led a healthy lifestyle—to this day, I go to the gym five to six times a week with joy and energy. The problem is that I was depressed most of the time. I wondered if I was crazy or ungrateful. How could I be depressed when I had the man of my dreams next me, and when I was so successful in my work? It did not make sense to me, and I knew that it had to relate to a chemical imbalance in my body. I did all the possible blood tests and my doctors said my results were normal. I decided to check my health with a doctor who has an unconventional way of thinking when it comes to medicine and the functions of the body. When I went to the doctor—who was a friend of my sister—I told her that I knew there was something wrong with me and I requested all kinds of blood tests to figure it out.

Finally, over a month later, I received my results. The doctor found a reason—actually, two reasons. First, my thyroid numbers showed that I had clear hypothyroidism. My previous doctors who had told me that my numbers were normal had actually been using an old method for reference. The new doctor said it was clear that, for my age and lifestyle, this couldn't be normal. Secondly, I had high levels of toxicity in my body, which put me at higher risk to get cancer. She put me on thyroid medicine, a diet program and supplements to natu-rally cleanse my body of the toxins. I can't tell you how happy I was to get back to my normal self again. I started to sleep better without anxiety attacks, my skin changed, I started to lose the excess weight, eventually getting back to my normal size.

It felt like I had been imprisoned and was finally set free. With better sleeping habits and less anxiety, I started to feel better about myself and I started to shine more at my job. My face and my energy said it all; I know how health can change everything. I know the value of an excellent night's sleep. I know how it feels to wake up, look in the mirror and see a rested face with a big smile that appears without effort.

Based on my journey and purpose, I wanted to offer readers some suggestions and reminders to help them take care of themselves. Showing love and respect to yourself is the foundation of building your brand. Start your personal brand when you are content and happy with yourself; it's your time to shine with confidence to inspire others. Confidence is not created by fake emotions or heavy makeup; rather, it will show naturally on the face of someone who takes great care of themselves. Here are a few recommendations that will help you to work on yourself and ignite your inner energy.

Your Body | It's incredible how exercise can change your reality and mood. I would put sports at the top of the list of any mood enhancers —working out releases endorphins that give you a natural feeling of elation. At first, I used to go to the gym as if it were an obligation to stay fit and not gain weight. After many years of personal training and fitness classes, I realized that I go to these because I really love myself and my body, and it makes me feel great. Yes, there are many days when I don't feel particularly motivated to exercise. I used to take breaks from working out, especially on vacation. But the day I skip going to the gym is the day I lose my energy. I encourage you all to exercise—whether that means finding a gym or creating one at home —so that you can get into the zone of working out.

You don't need to wake up at 5 A.M. to run or exercise, but you should commit to adding some form of exercise into your daily sched- ule. Any type of physical activity can enhance your mood and protect your health in the future. Find someone who is willing to join you so you can encourage each other. Join fitness classes that you like, or try a new activity—it's never too late to try something you've never done before.

Food is another major factor in protecting your health. Throughout my life, I have tried many fad diets. I now realize that the secret is balance. I came to the decision that I wouldn't deprive myself, yet I would control my cravings. I eat a little of everything and I fast for 16 hours. I stopped consuming certain foods that could exacerbate my thyroid condition. Other than that, I eat balanced meals without binging. It's important to personalize your diet for your own health needs—what works for one person might not work for someone else, depending on allergies, health conditions, lifestyle, personal preferences, culture, and other factors. You can take a simple blood test to discover any food allergies and sensitivities; then you can eliminate these items. Again, the type of healthy diet you want to follow is your choice. Just stay away from junk food and any food item that will poison your blood with heavy metals and toxins.

Your Mind | The year 2020 came with many strange circumstances. The lockdown, the stressful news of the pandemic, and not being able to see friends and family members put the mental health of so many people worldwide to the test—and I am certainly included in this group. I went through another wave of depression; I wasn't able to grow, and I couldn't see things clearly. But despite all of that, I loved 2020 because it brought me so much gratitude for those moments of truth and all the skills that I learned. I had to pull myself up and find my way back to productivity. I started to push myself to stay happy and fight any negativity. I had a few sessions of therapy, but I know that it was not the only solution. The real help comes from within; I had to pull myself up. I finally made it, and I started writing this book. I had to do a lot of affirmation talks before going to sleep. All of the affirmations and visualization worked because I believed in myself.

I am a person who struggles with meditation with its conventional methods. If you feel the same way, then you understand what I mean. I believe in the power of meditation; I just felt that I needed to find my own way to relax my brain. I feel that my type of meditation is different; it comes from physical activities like sports and dancing. Cooking, to my surprise, helps to clear my mind as well. I highly encourage you to find your own way of programming to put your mind in a positive and balanced state. Of course, I know that some people have medical conditions, and they need to address them before going through this self-talk. Please make sure that you are working with a doctor or other medical professional to manage your physical conditions before you're ready to explore the beauty of your mind.

I advise you to be responsible for your emotions and never blame others or outside circumstances for your difficulties. You are responsible for creating your own happiness as well. Taking care of yourself is part of the journey, and it will be a transition period until you are able to live your purpose. Maybe your partner or friends won't understand what you're going through. Maybe they will not know how to deal with you. That transition phase might make you look like someone that they do not know. Just keep growing and taking care of yourself; you deserve it. Create your moment to shine. Every night, continue to train your brain to think about wonderful things and all of the blessings you have. To put it simply, train yourself to be grateful. Once your body and your mind are healthy, all people around you will be amazed and happy. Only then will they appreciate your journey and what you had to experience.

One of the things that has always helped me stay hopeful is to imagine achieving my goal. Picturing positive images is a technique that has a magical effect on the mind. Imagine yourself standing on a stage and delivering a TED talk in front of thousands of people. You are there speaking and encouraging an entire generation to live a healthy and happy life. I actually consistently kept this image in my mind until I was invited to become TEDx speaker. I did it and I stood there shining, just as I had imagined.

Growth and Skill Development | I used to picture myself attending one of Brendon Burchard's training sessions in the United States. I tried to register and book my seat twice, but I stopped. I would reach the checkout button and then just leave the website. I was putting other priorities first. We were building our house and had many expenses; we were still paying rent and having other financial responsibilities, so the training sessions seemed like too big of a financial investment at the time. But one day I asked my husband if it would be all right to invest this money into my self-development. He agreed immediately, saying that it would make me happy, which in turn would make him happy, knowing that I was investing in myself. He even gave me his airline miles so that I could upgrade my ticket and fly business class for the 16-hour flight. Everything happened so fast. I always knew that I would grow massively if I could be around this amazing network. I knew that I would go one day—I even put it on my vision board. It was the right time when I made it a priority.

Make your growth and your development a priority. Decorating a room in your house or taking a short vacation can wait. If it doesn't affect your health or your significant relationships, then make your growth a priority. You will always have obligations, time restrictions, and financial responsibilities; that's life. But you deserve to invest in yourself and to work towards a shining future. You need a healthy mind that leads your growth. Once you have clarity about your goals, you will be ready to move forward. A clear mind is a healthy and free mind. When you grow, your giving back to the universe will grow as well. You will be able to serve with more confidence and maturity.

Skills development is another blessing of 2020 and the lockdown. I believe it created massive success for online training platforms. It was the right time to start to think about gaining new skills or working on a weakness. For your personal brand, you need to identify your communication weaknesses. You don't need a year of pandemic and lockdown to start building your skills—you just need to add it to your list of priorities. You need to plan for it.

In Kuwait, I was approached by a sweet lady who works as an interior designer. She was doing a great job in her career, and I saw amazing potential for growth in her story. She needed my help to build her personal brand. She had one issue: not being comfortable in front of the camera. I told her that a personal brand would not be personal if it was solely about work; she needed to put herself into it as well. She was fine with a voice-over or a video that would show only her hands while she was designing, but I offered to help and train her on standing and speaking in front of the camera. She was not convinced and refused to develop her communication skills, a decision that I totally respected and understood. Today, I have no doubt that she is achieving amazing goals in her career. But maybe, at that time, she was not ready to fix a weakness in her communication skills, and she was not ready to start a personal brand just yet.

It's a commitment that we all have to make. There are essentials and principles for each career path that we take. We cannot cut it short. We have to take the full journey and accept our responsibilities. I recommend that you conduct some kind of situational analysis, where you list all of your strengths and weaknesses, and start there. Identify the primary skills that you need to develop. For personal brands, you definitely need to work on communication. Once you establish your brand, you can develop other skills, such as persuasion. You don't have to be an expert in digital marketing nor social media management, but you need to know the basic concepts in order to establish your brand. Pick the set of skills that will help you establish your personal brand and remember that you don't have to do every-thing by yourself. There are other people who believe in your purpose and are willing to help you.

Relationships | We need our loved ones to surround and support us. Remember that you want to represent a role model for future generations, so be your authentic self and present your real emotions. Taking care of your significant relationships is a crucial factor in the health of you psychological and social state. Your partner or signifi-cant other needs to feel comfortable with you being in the spotlight, because they will be there with you as well.

Your friends are your chosen family, and they deserve for you to make more time for them. In my circle of friends, I was always the one who was away and busy. I missed many great gatherings and occasions. One day I realized that I was starting to exit their lives, and that hurt me so much. They were always talking about issues that I did not know about. They would laugh, recalling stories and encounters that I didn't understand. I felt the distance and realized that I needed to fix my behavior and start to designate more time for my friends. Spending time with those you love and care about—laughing together, traveling together, and creating memories together is extremely important. Make your partner feel that they are at the top of your priorities because they are your partner in life and their happiness is tied to your happiness. Take care of your children and become their best friend. These amazing relationships will be your army to face life and walk the steps in your journey. They are your forever supports; never the obstacles.

Chapter Takeaways

I wanted to share some of my very personal stories to let you know that you should come first. Your personal brand will be of no use if you are not taking good care of yourself. Your audience will feel and sense your energy and your vibes. You can be going through a lot of difficulties in your life—fighting a painful disease, or even striving for a good cause—

but you will always need to work on yourself first. At the end of the day, it's *your* brand—it is about you and your influence on others. You need to deliver your influence with complete belief in your cause and fresh outlook on life; this happens once you have a healthy mind and calm spirit. You will be able to reach this point of comfort with your story and your brand only when you start taking good care of yourself.

I offered my recommendations in taking care of your body, mind, growth and skill development, and relationships. You want to shine and inspire others, and this will happen when you care about your health and commit to living a healthy lifestyle. Your mind needs to be clear from all depressing thoughts, and that's why your mental health and ways of thinking need to reflect peace and optimism. Even if you have the strongest, most touching story, you will still need to develop your communication skills or build new skills to be able to share your story the right way, with the right audience. Be honest with yourself and work on your weaknesses as that is what will help you to succeed in your personal brand, or in any future endeavor. Finally, my advice for you is to always remember that you are not living alone, nor should die alone. Our relationships are treasures that we collect over the years. We need to take care of these relationships and make sure that our personal brand is not going to affect these relationships.

Chapter Activity

The last activity in this book is about being honest about your strengths and weaknesses. Create a general check-up on yourself. The health of your body, your mind, and your soul is very important. Here is a worksheet that might help you:

1. What are your major health issues and what is your plan to deal with them? *(example: I have high blood pressure and I need to fix my diet and become more active)*

_____

_____

2. What is your plan to maintain a healthier lifestyle? *(example: sleeping early, reducing sugar in my diet, being physically active several times a week...)*

_____

_____

3. What is your plan for a healthier mind? *(example: meditate more to deal with stress and anxiety, use more positive affirmation)*

_____

_____

4. How can you maintain healthy relationships with your loved ones? *(Example: visit family more often, make time for friends, enhance communication with my partner)*

_____

_____

5. What is your plan for growth and self-development?

_____

_____

6. List the strengths that you want to enhance and the weaknesses that you want to fix and your plan for achieving this goal.

STRENGTHS	WEAKNESSES
1. Strong and impactful story: I need to work on linking this story to my purpose and turn it into content that inspires others. Maybe I should hire a copy writer to help me.	1. I cannot speak in public: I will consider joining workshops to help me with this kind of anxiety. Maybe I should find a coach or a mentor to help me.

Conclusion

In writing this book, I wanted to bring some light to many young individuals that have committed suicide, felt a severe loss of self-confidence or have lost track of their values and ethics. Social media platforms are full of famous people who are hungry for more "likes" and followers, so they can sell ideas and products that have no real value. They are paid to make people crave more materialistic things and look for fake beauty. These words are coming from a marketing expert who is so sorry that her profession is used to misguide many societies around the world. Influencers are a great marketing channels and there is so much potential for the growth of this industry—but I have a hard time digesting the social effect that some of these influencers have on the younger generations. People are unhappy with their looks. They are no longer seeing the value of education, and are instead looking for sources of easy money through marketing and influencing hundreds or thousands of followers.

As a woman who has always dreamt big, it's not fair to judge the young for following the steps of influencers without offering them an alternative of "good famous." The world is full of amazing achievers and real-life heroes who are rarely mentioned, or never seen.

Being a social person, I get to meet new people all the time. Some of the people I meet are great role models, but they do not know how to reach the younger segment of our population. Professionals, scientists, trauma survivors, or people who are fighting now for the sake of freedom and justice are all great examples of the "good famous" I am referring to. Many of them have amazing stories, but they don't know how to start telling them in order to reach those who need them the most.

In this book, I wanted to offer a formula for anyone who believes they can inspire and motivate others by building a successful brand. I am offering a complete guide on how to prepare and launch your personal brand. There are many agencies that offer marketing and PR services to help you disseminate your content, but there is a gap that you need to fill first. Before taking a beautiful professional photo and posting it on Instagram, you have to prepare yourself for fame and for a professional personal brand. Before formatting your unique logo, you need to work on yourself first and think about your marketing plan.

At the start of this book, I explained the importance of finding your purpose and how to find the story that you will share with your audience. Our story and purpose are usually in front of our eyes, but we cannot see them. By enlisting friends to assist in describing who we are, we are able to discover the unique tools and skills that make us shine.

To succeed in a personal brand, you will always need a story that is related to what your audience is going through, and the key is authenticity. Do not ever lie about your story or try to fabricate the details. Your story should be a real one and should represent how you will use it to live your purpose.

Once you've identified your story, it's time to face your enemies. The enemies are the excuses that people use to delay the state of living your purpose. In the second chapter, I discussed many excuses such as "lack of time" and "lack of skills." I want to make it clear that it's normal to postpone a major shift in your life because of an enemy idea inside your head. The most important thing is to always remember that you *deserve* to shine and succeed. Your audience is waiting for you; they want to hear your story as it might save them a lot of agony and effort, just by following in your footsteps. For the next five chapters, I introduced my formula for the success of personal brands. The first element of the formula—the first step towards your success—is to start somewhere. Plan your steps and know where you are going. You should not be in a rush as you are working towards living your purpose. You have a message to deliver, so don't waste it—make sure that you plan to spread it the right way.

The fourth chapter is about your competition on the journey of living the purpose. You should not allow the concept of competition to distract or scare you. Competition will always be there and it will not affect your uniqueness. You are not a product that you can be copied; you are a human being with your own unique feelings and experiences. The concept of competition is an encouragement agent for you to grow and work hard to deliver your message. Try not to compare yourself to others; you are special the way you are.

The fifth chapter discusses the third element of the formula: how to think about yourself as a brand. This is when you think about your personal brand as the ID card that introduces you to the public. It is your passport to access and inspire others. When they hear your name, they will immediately think about your story and how motivating you are.

The sixth chapter is an introduction to the main concepts of marketing and how you can utilize them to succeed in your personal brand. It is not particularly useful to your personal brand to ask an agency to help you without you knowing the basics.

Finally, the last chapter of the book focuses on the importance of taking care of yourself. Taking care of yourself is the foundation for succeeding in your personal brand; the health of your body, mind, relationships, and skills are the main pillars that will help you lead a healthy and energetic life.

In each chapter, I offered worksheets that you can use on a regular basis to truly focus on your purpose. Each chapter's activities are suggested guidelines for you to prepare for establishing your personal brand. Feel free to use them as you wish; I am sure that you will be able to add to them once you realize their importance.

I am very happy and proud to be writing this conclusion. I spent many nights blaming myself for letting the day go by without writing a single word. Today, I am concluding it. I believe that this is the right time for me to become an author. It feels right and I am very content and grateful. Most importantly, I want to end my first book with two words: pride and gratitude.

Samar M. Baqer
    @DrSamarBaqer
    sambaqer@gmail.com

Best
Sellers
Academy

This book was published with the support of The Legacy Project.

Do you have a book on the inside of you?

Let us serve as your midwives to help you give birth to your
international bestselling book!

Phone: 1-678-842-4346
Email: success@thebestsellersacademy.com
Website: TheBestsellersAcademy.com